Engaging Conversations
For Couples

Christ-honoring Conversation Starters
For a Closer Connection

.

Jed Jurchenko

www.CoffeeShopConversations.com

© 2017 by Jed Jurchenko.

Printed by CreateSpace,
An Amazon.com Company
Available from Amazon.com

Highly engaging, Christ-honoring conversation starters to grow your relationship and deepen your connection.

Also By Jed

131 Creative Conversations for Couples

131 Necessary Conversations before Marriage

131 Creative Conversations for Families

131 Conversations for Stepfamily Success

131 Conversations that Engage Kids

131 Boredom Busters and Creativity Builders

131 Stress Busters and Mood Boosters for Kids

Coffee Shop Conversations: Psychology and the Bible

Coffee Shop Inspirations: Simple Strategies for Building Dynamic Leadership and Relationships

Unlocking Stepfamily Success eCourse

Get Free Books!

To thank you for your purchase, I would like to send you a free gift.

Transform from discouraged and burned out, to an enthusiastic agent of joy who leads at a higher–happier–level! *Be Happier Now*, is perfect for parents, stepparents, mentors, pastors, coaches, and friends. You will discover practical strategies for staying energized so that you can encourage and refresh others.

I will also make sure that you are the first to know about free book launches and new releases!

www.coffeeshopconversations.com/happiness/

Dedication

To my wife, Jenny. Thank you for the many, incredible, date experiences. The evenings spent sipping coffee, asking great questions, and dreaming about our future together, are among my favorite memories. The fun, adventure, love, and friendship that you add to my life is astounding!

To my daughters Mackenzie, Brooklyn, Addison, and Emma. You added an overwhelming amount of joy to my life, and I love each of you! Although you four are a long way away from dating and marriage, my prayer is that, when the time is right, you will experience the joy that comes from finding a best friend, with whom you can share your inner world.

Contents

Connection Secrets of Happy Couples

Envision waking up next to the person you care about most in the world. Imagine how it would feel to traverse through life, hand-in-hand, with your best friend. This person is aware of your successes, failures, hopes, dreams, and fears. Yet, in spite of all of these things, and because of these things, he or she loves you deeply. In short, the two of you are profoundly connected.

Naturally, this type of bond does not mean the two of you see eye-to-eye on everything. Yet, you find this perfectly acceptable. Opposites attract, and if you both always had the same outlook, then one of you would not be necessary. For this reason, in your relationship, differences are celebrated.

One of the best parts about your connection is its steadiness. Yours is not a relational rollercoaster, where moments of closeness are interrupted by fiery rage or icy coldness. Instead, you are reliable confidants who are always on each other's side.

Of course, your relationship is not seven days a week of nonstop bliss–that would be exhausting. Instead, it is more like a cozy sweater that you can always count on for comfort and warmth. There is a peace that comes from knowing you could make a dumb mistake–even an extraordinarily dumb mistake–and your partner would welcome you with open arms, stating, "Honey, I am so sorry this happened."

Five years from now, the two of you will continue to be madly in love. You believe this with all of your heart. Fifty years from now, you can picture yourselves strolling, hand-in-hand through the park. For some, a truly happy relationship sounds too good to be true. Fortunately, a close connection like the one described is not reserved for fairytales. It is available to every couple willing to learn to connect in three significant ways.

The Secret of Happy Relationships

Happy, secure relationships do not happen by accident. These couples have a secret to their success. They know how to connect well. This is accomplished by connecting often, connecting intimately, and reconnecting quickly whenever a disruption occurs. These three connection principles are the foundation of nearly every happy relationship.

The goal of this book is to support you and your partner in connecting in each of these vital ways. I use the term partner because this book is for all couples. I am a firm believer that it is never too early, nor too late to strengthen your bond. Whether you are on your first date, approaching your golden anniversary, or somewhere in between, these conversation starters are designed to assist you in drawing closer together than ever before.

Like exercising to build muscle mass, the connection to our loved one grows with intentional effort. On the other hand, if you and I lounge in front of the television, gorge on potato chips, and act as though our partner does not exist, then our connection will slowly wither away. This book is for couples who are willing to take action by exercising their connection muscles. Before diving into the conversations, let's first examine what connection is, and why each of the three connection components is vital.

Connection Defined

I define connection as any activity that causes you and your partner to draw closer together. If feelings of love, warmth, and friendship increase, then a connecting moment has occurred. To understand the value of connectedness, it may help to visualize a love-bank built into your partner's heart. Love-bank deposits are made every time your partner feels cared for. On the other hand, when he or she feels disrespected, taken for granted, hurt, or unloved, then a love-bank withdrawal occurs.

It is important to note that love-bank deposits and withdrawals center around your partner's feelings. They are not based on your intentions. If your loved one feels disrespected, then you have made a withdrawal, even if your motives were pure. Positive and negative transactions are a normal part of all relationships. Similar to traditional banking, love-bank goals should include making regular deposits, building a healthy savings, and never allowing one's balance to fall into the negative. In love-banking terms, a zero-balance means that your partner no longer feels valued by you, and this is a perilous state for any relationship.

It is important to note that the love-bank is not a method of keeping score. Nor is it a tit-for-tat mentality that says, "I did something nice for you, so later, you must return the favor." Instead, the love-bank metaphor is a vivid reminder that the people we care about will not feel valued if we do not act in loving ways toward them. Remember, love is an action word.

The skills of connecting often, connecting intimately, and reconnecting quickly are strategies that happy couples employ to fill each other's love-banks. Now, let's explore why each of these three areas is vital to a healthy, vibrant relationship.

Happy Couples Connect Often

A common relationship myth is that high-quality interactions make up for the lack of significant time together. It is the age-old debate of whether quality time or quantity time together is most important. The bottom line is that both are necessary, and the two cannot be separated. Powerful connection moments happen when we least expect them, which is why connecting often is essential.

Years ago, before Jenny and I married, the two of us went hiking down a long stretch of deserted beach. Five miles into our trek, we paused for a picnic lunch. Afterward, we headed back to our car. Up to this point, the trip was pleasant. However, it was at the tail end of our journey that the big magic happened.

Suddenly, a pod of dolphin came bounding through the waves, less than fifty feet from shore. Jenny and I were ecstatic and paused to take in the moment. We assumed the dolphins would pass by quickly, but they didn't. Apparently, they were as enthralled by us as we were by them. When we resumed our stroll, the dolphins followed along, keeping perfect time. They entertained themselves by jumping over waves and enchanted us with their chatter. Finally, after a good deal of time had passed, the dolphins swam off toward the setting sun.

Magical moments like this simply cannot be planned. Our hike down the beach turned into an extraordinarily joyful memory and a powerful moment of connection that Jenny and I will forever cherish. I share this simple story because it illustrates why connecting often is necessary.

Designed to Connect

You and I are God-designed to connect. The book of Genesis describes how, after creating the heavens and the earth, God brought every animal before Adam, in what appears to be the very first relational experiment. Adam named each pair of beasts and noted that none was fit to be his lifelong companion. Then, God stated, "It is not good for the man to be alone. I will make a companion for him who corresponds to him."[1] God caused Adam to fall into a deep sleep before fashioning Eve, the first woman, out of Adam's own rib. The bottom line is that you and I are hardwired by God to connect.

Strategies for Connecting Often

Some couples connect by carving out large chunks of time together all at once. Others orchestrate small, frequent interactions throughout the day. The important thing is to keep the positive exchanges flowing. Connecting builds trust. It is also when hilarious inside jokes form, and where deep conversations flow naturally.

In connecting often, remember that feelings follow actions. On days you are tired, frustrated, or simply do not feel like putting forth the effort, try laying your protests aside and connecting anyway.

Likely, it will not be long before the two of you are having a blast!

As you move through this book, you will notice that some conversation starters are purely for fun. There is an important reason for this. Not every conversation needs to have a purpose. If the two of you are connecting, solely for the joy of connecting, then you are doing things right. Be a couple that makes connecting the norm, because this is how lasting love forms.

Happy Couples Connect Intimately

Although society sometimes associates the word intimacy with sex, this is not how it is used in this book. None of the conversations are intended to make you blush. Instead, intimacy is defined as in-to-me-see. It is the ability to know our partner deeply while simultaneously allowing ourselves to be known.

Intimacy forms through a mutual sharing of hopes, dreams, fears, and failures. Being fully known, and fully loved is powerful. It allows us to run toward our partner instead of away from him or her during times of distress.

For me, intimacy is a game changer. As a busy daddy of four girls, I get scatterbrained often, and goofs are far more common than I would like to admit. Not long ago, I shuttled our two older girls from their slumber parties, to soccer games, and ice-skating lessons. Along the way, the girls and I stopped at home for lunch. Before rushing inside, I gathered an armful of garbage from the van−the kind of trash that endlessly appears out of nowhere when kids are around. Unfortunately, in my haste to clean, I inadvertently dropped our keys into the garbage bin.

It was not until after lunch that I realized that the keys were missing. This resulted in an all-out family search. Fortunately, after much hunting, the missing keys were found, and the girls made it to their next event, albeit slightly late. The bright side of this whole debacle is that I was able to freely own up to my mistake. Never did I feel like I needed to try to cover up my blunder. Later that evening, Jenny and I laughed about the incident.

Jenny reminded me that, in the scheme of things, momentarily losing our keys in the garbage is not that bad. She recalled how she left a previous set of keys on our van roof. As our family cruised down the highway, a compassionate driver pulled alongside us. In one hand, he held up a single key that he had removed from his keychain, as he feverishly pointed to the roof. Although we took the next exit, it was too late. Our keys were long gone.

In our home, goofs are common. Fortunately, so is grace. Intimacy is all about grace. It says, "I know you. I see who you are, and I love you—mistakes and all."

God-Designed for Intimacy

Romans 5:8 says, "But God demonstrates his own love for us, in that while we were still sinners, Christ died for us." You and I are fully known, fully accepted, and fully loved by God. This is intimacy at its best.

Intimate relationships are the safest place to be. Some of the conversation starters in this book are designed to stir up intimacy by helping you peer into your partner's hopes, dreams, fears, and failures. As you move through the questions, lay aside the desire to change your partner, and to fix longstanding issues. Instead, get curious. Listen with empathy. Ask good follow-up questions, and whenever possible, accept your partner for whom he or she is. Doing this is precisely what will take your relationship to a deeper level.

Happy Couples Reconnect Quickly

According to marriage researcher John Gottman, happy couples excel at repair attempts.[2] Repair attempts are what allow couples to reconnect quickly after a relational disruption. One might say that happy couples know how to connect like Velcro.

If you take a close look at this unique fabric, you will notice that one side contains many minute hooks, while the other side has an abundance of tiny loops on which these hooks fasten. As a child, I remember being fascinated by Velcro. I would see how close I could place the strips to each other before they would begin to connect. Apparently, some of the hooks and loops stretch out further than the others do, because the entire system joins almost magically. It is as if the hooks and loops reach out for each other.

This is exactly how happy couples connect and reconnect—they reach for each other. This might happen through a shared joke, gentle touch, kind gesture, or a soft smile. The specific technique a couple uses to reconnect is unimportant. What matters is that each person actively seeks to reestablish the bond. Unhappy couples take the opposite approach. They return unkind gesture for unkind gesture, spiraling into an escalating pattern of love-bank withdrawals.

Happy and Unhappy Couples in Action

Now, let's take a look at happy couples and unhappy couples in action. A common, unhappy interaction will look like this: She makes a negative statement. He reacts by rolling his eyes. She counters with a critical remark. He feels overwhelmed and shuts down. This pattern continues for hours, days, weeks, or even years. Both partners push each other away, and each is miserable.

Happy couples implement simple repair attempts that disrupt this pattern. Let's look at one way a happy couple might utilize a repair attempt to reconnect. The scenario begins the same: She makes a negative comment. He rolls his eyes. She begins to counter with a critical comment but catches herself. Instead, she rolls her eyes back, while sticking out her tongue, and making a silly face–this is the repair attempt. He smiles back and makes an even more ridiculous face in return–thus receiving and reciprocating the repair attempt. At this point, the couple bursts into outrageous laughter. They have reached an unspoken agreement to cease the love-bank withdraws and to reunite.

Diving Deeper into Reconnection

In regards to the previous scenario, a quick word of caution is necessary. Eye rolling and silly faces will not work for every couple. Some people would view these gestures as additional insults. Thus, it is necessary to find repair attempts that fit the personality of you and your partner. In this case, the man knows that rolling his eyes is rude. When the woman rolls her eyes and makes a silly face in return, she is communicating, "I see you trying to be hurtful, but instead of making an issue about this, I am going to let go of my hurt and make a joke." He reciprocates, nonverbally communicating, "I like your humor, and I am willing to let go of my hurt too."

Reconnecting and Scripture

In Ephesians 4:26, the Bible affirms the value of being quick to forgive. This passage states, "Be angry and do not sin; do not let the sun go down on the cause of your anger." As you will see, some of the questions in this book hone-in on reconnecting during the stressful moments of life. While happy couples are not connected all of the time, they are connected most of the time. They excel at repair attempts, connecting like Velcro, by reaching out to each other after relational disruptions occur.

Christ, the Connection Foundation

You may have noticed that each of these connection principles is grounded in Scripture. This is because God knows how we function best. Thus, making Christ the center of your relationship is vital. He is the foundation on which each connection principles rests.

Colossians 4:6 says, "Let your speech always be gracious, seasoned with salt." As you progress through this book, season all of your conversations with grace. Be patient with each other, have fun, and enjoy the process. Wishing you many happy conversations in the pages ahead!

Sincerely,

COFFEE SHOP CONVERSATIONS

131
Engaging Conversations
For Couples

To be fully seen by somebody, then, and be loved anyhow–this is a human offering that can border on miraculous.

~ Elizabeth Gilbert,

You know you're in love when you can't fall asleep because reality is finally better than your dreams.

~ Dr. Seuss

Two people are better than one.

~ Ecclesiastes 4:9a

Question #1

Imagine that you have the opportunity to grant your partner a superpower. What superhuman ability would you bestow upon him or her, and why?

Question #2

The doctor informs you that you must eliminate either caffeine or sugar from your diet. Which do you get rid of, and why?

Question #3

Describe a happy childhood memory from a camp, trip, or sleepover. Then, share what made this experience so memorable.

Question #4

Similar to the movie *Supersize Me*, you will dine off the menu of a single fast food restaurant for an entire month. Fortunately, you get to choose which eatery this will be. Which restaurant do you select, and why?

Question #5

If you had to relocate to a different state, where would you move, and why?

Question #6

Imagine that you must shut down all of your social media accounts but one. Which accounts would you close? Which site would you continue using? Then, explain why?

Question #7

You can turn invisible. You can go anywhere, and do anything, completely unseen. How will you use this superpower?

Question #8

Imagine that you find a wallet. Inside are a photo identification card and five, $100 bills. No one is watching. What will you do with the wallet, i.d. card, and money? Explain the reasons behind your decision.

Question #9

Would you rather go skydiving, scuba diving, or relax at home? Why?

Question #10

Complete this sentence, "The three apps on my phone that I can't live without are..."

Question #11

Describe a time during your childhood when you felt especially close to God. Where were you, what happened, and what was this feeling like?

Question #12

What current activities, events, or people help you to feel closer to God?

Question #13

Describe a childhood event that left you with a negative view of God. First, describe what happened, then share how this affected you, personally.

Question #14

Now, describe a current event that left you with a positive view of God. First, tell what happened, and then share how this event contributed to your understanding of God or grew your faith in Him.

Question #15

Imagine, that like in the movie *Groundhog Day*, you will relive the same day, over and over again. What day was so amazing that you would repeat it?

Question #16

George Bernard Shaw said, "If you cannot get rid of the family skeleton, you may as well make it dance." Describe a family skeleton from your childhood.

Question #17

Tell about a time you put Shaw's advice into action and made a family skeleton dance by using a current challenge for good.

Question #18

Describe a current family skeleton. In your opinion, why is this tricky issue hidden away and not talked about openly?

Question #19

What current family skeleton could you creatively use to your advantage? How might you accomplish this?

Question #20

Randy Pausch, the author of *The Last Lecture*,[3] writes, "The brick walls are not there to keep us out. The brick walls are there to give us a chance to show how badly we want something. Because the brick walls are there to stop the people who don't want it badly enough. They're there to stop the other people." Do you agree or disagree with Randy's statement, and why?

Question #21

Describe a time in your life when a brick wall caused you to press forward harder, which led to achieving your goal.

Question #22

Describe a current brick wall you are facing at home, work, or school. How would it feel to overcome this obstacle?

Question #23

What are some ways that your partner can support you in overcoming your current brick wall challenges?

Question #24

When facing the brick walls in your life, would you describe yourself as easily discouraged, someone who persistently presses forward in spite of challenges, or are you somewhere in between? Then, explain why you see yourself this way.

Question #25

In your family, who excels at optimistically pressing forward in the midst of challenging circumstances? What do you think is the secret behind this person's persistence?

Question #26

The Pareto Principle, also known as the 80/20 rule, states that roughly 80% of results come from 20% of our efforts, while 80% of the work we do accounts for a mere 20% of the results. The Pareto Principle is often applied in business, relationships, and life. It is a reminder to focus on the tasks that matter most. Have you heard of this principle before, and what is your overall impression of the concept?

Question #27

In your relationship, what do you consider to be the 20% activities or the ones that draw the two of you the closest together?

Question #28

Complete this sentence, "When you ____, I am blown away by your love for me."

Question #29

Thinking back over your relationship, describe a time when you felt incredibly loved by your partner. What, made this moment so meaningful to you?

Question #30

If your partner wanted to make you feel especially loved today, what types of things should he or she do?

Question #31

According to Pareto, 20% of our daily activities account for nearly 80% of the joy in our life. In regards to happiness, fun, and joy what are some of your 20% activities?

Question #32

When you and your partner are having fun as a couple, what activities bring you the most joy?

Question #33

What are some couples activities that bring you less joy, but that you continue to engage in because you know that it means a lot to your partner?

Question #34

A study reports that some thirteen-year-olds check their social media accounts as much as 100 times a day.[4] How often do you check your social media accounts? How important is social media to your everyday life?

Question #35

Surprise, you are about to contract a mental illness. On the bright side, you get to choose which illness this will be. Which do you pick, and why?

Question #36

Which mental illness frightens you the most, and why?

Question #37

If a loved one suspected you were showing signs of mental illness, how would you want this brought to your attention? How would you want your partner to care for you during this time?

Question #38

Who, in your family, exhibits signs of mental illness? In what ways has this affected your relationship with this person and your life in general?

Question #39

"Trauma is a life-organizing event."[5] This means that painful events from our past can influence the way we interact with others and view the world. Describe a past event that continues to affect you today. Tell what happened, and how the event changed you.

Question #40

Describe someone you know who is stuck in past pain. What do you think caused him or her to get stuck? How are you an encouragement to this person?

Question #41

Who do you know that has overcome a painful past? What are some of the qualities that might have allowed this person to push past adversity?

Question #42

In regards to trauma, how would you currently describe yourself? Are you stuck in past hurt? Are you in the process of working through the pain, or would you describe yourself as fully recovered from old wounds?

Question #43

If your partner notices that you are having an exceptionally difficult day, how would you want him or her to support you?

Question #44

Children have excellent imaginations. Describe a childhood game or activity that delighted you and your friends.

Question #45

Imagine the pastor of your church asks you to preach a sermon on any topic that you are passionate about. What would the theme of your sermon be?

Question #46

What is one piece of wisdom, given to you by a parent, teacher, coach, or mentor, that has stuck with you over time? Why do you think these words have been so meaningful?

Question #47

Imagine that you are asked to give advice to a newly dating couple. What words of wisdom would you share, and why?

Question #48

When is the last time you laughed aloud, and what made you laugh?

Question #49

Describe something you admire about your grandparents.

Question #50

Describe a quality that you admire in your parents.

Question #51

Most kids try a variety of sports, clubs, and extracurricular activities throughout their childhood. Describe a childhood activity that you gave up, but now wish that you didn't. What was it about this activity that brought you joy?

Question #52

Growing up, what were your biggest pet peeves?

Question #53

Describe your happiest moment over the past week. Why did this moment bring you so much joy?

Question #54

Looking over the past week, describe your greatest disappointment. What made this time so discouraging?

Question #55

Describe a favorite rainy day memory or rainy day activity from childhood.

Question #56

Imagine that you and your partner are stuck indoors during a thunderstorm. Then, describe what the perfect rainy day date would look like.

Question #57

It has been said that "Children may forget what you say, but they will never forget how you made them feel."[6] What childhood mentor, teacher, or friend made you feel especially important?

Question #58

What specific actions do you take to make the people around you feel valued?

Question #59

Describe a time during the past week that your partner made you feel important. What did he or she do, and why did this mean so much to you?

Question #60

If you could travel back in time and witness a Biblical miracle, which miracle would you most like to see?

Question #61

Describe a happy memory from your early twenties. Where were you, who were you with, and what happened?

Question #62

Describe a major disappointment from your early twenties.

Question #63

If you had the opportunity to travel back in time and talk to your twenty-year-old self, what advice would you give?

Question #64

If your twenty-year-old self were to travel into the future and meet you today, what might he or she think? Would your twenty-year-old self be thrilled, disappointed, perplexed, etc.? Why?

Question #65

If you could return to college and study any subject, what would it be, and why?

Question #66

In 2 Peter 3:16, the Apostle Peter states that some things in Scripture are difficult to understand. What is one Biblical concept that confuses or frustrates you?

Question #67

What Biblical passage inspires you the most? Why do these verses mean so much to you, personally?

All you need is love.
But a little chocolate now and then doesn't hurt.

~Charles Schulz

Question #68

Marriage researcher, John Gottman, writes about the importance of repair attempts, or simple actions that reunite a couple after a quarrel. What repair attempts do you use to reconnect with your partner?

Question #69

How good are you at receiving your partner's repair attempts when he or she tries to reconnect? First, describe what you do well. Then, explain what you could do better.

Question #70

On a scale of 1-10, how good are you and your partner at reconnecting after a disagreement? Then, explain why you assigned this number.

Question #71

What steps could your partner take to make reconnecting after a disagreement easier for you?

Question #72

The next time you are upset, what would you like to do to better manage your feelings of anger, hurt, and sadness?

Question #73

As a child, what did you imagine falling in love would be like?

Question #74

As an adult, how do you know that you are in love?

Question #75

What movie did you dislike so much that you would un-watch it if you could?

Question #76

Imagine a romantic comedy, based on your relationship, is being filmed. The director needs a fresh story for a funny, romantic scene. Which story do you tell?

Question #77

What movie do you consider to be the most romantic movie of all time, and why?

Question #78

A popular axiom proclaims, "A happy wife is a happy life." Do you agree with this statement? Why, or why not?

Question #79

Do you believe that the opposite is also true? Does an unhappy wife (or husband) result in an unhappy life? Then, explain your answer.

Question #80

What steps do you take to keep yourself happy throughout the day?

Question #81

How would you like your partner to contribute to your happiness? How good is he or she at doing the things you mentioned?

Question #82

In your opinion, what percentage of your happiness is your responsibility, and what percentage is your partner's responsibility? Then, explain the reasons for the numbers that you gave.

Question #83

Complete this sentence, "In marriage, a husband should always..."

Question #84

Finish this sentence, "In marriage, a husband should never..."

Question #85

Complete this sentence, "In marriage, a wife should always..."

Question #86

Finish this sentence, "In marriage, a wife should never..."

Question #87

Describe how your relationship with your partner has transformed you for the better.

Question #88

Finish this sentence, "If my 16-year-old self were to see me today, he or she would feel proud that..."

Question #89

Who do you consider to be a current mentor or role model? What do you admire about this person?

Question #90

Who are you currently mentoring–or who could you mentor–and what do you think this person could learn from you?

Question #91

What Biblical hero do you greatly admire, and why?

Question #92

What character qualities does this Biblical hero possess, that you would like to emulate?

Question #93

How old were you when you got your first cell phone? Then, tell the story of how you got it.

If you would be loved, love, and be loveable.

~ Benjamin Franklin

Question #94

1 John 4:17, states, "As He (Jesus) is, so are we in this world." How is Christ working through you, as His hands and feet in the world?

Question #95

Who is someone that is acting as Jesus' hands and feet in your life? First, tell who this person is, then share what he or she does that is so meaningful to you.

Question #96

If, you knew that you would lose your ability to hear tomorrow, how would you spend your last day of hearing? Who would you talk with, what songs would you play, etc.?

Question #97

What childhood cartoon or toy do you hope comes back in style?

Question #98

What do you consider the hardest thing you ever did? Would ever you do it again?

Question #99

What was your New Year's Resolution for this year, and how much progress have you made toward your goal?

Question #100

Which book, outside of the Bible, has grown your faith the most? What was your biggest take away from this book?

Question #101

In the 2006 comedy, *Click*, Michael Newman, played by Adam Sandler, obtains a universal remote control that allows him to fast-forward through the frustrating parts of his life. If you owned this remote, what parts of your life would you fast-forward through?

Question #102

If you owned a magical remote that allowed you to rewind your relationship and change something from the past, what would do differently?

Question #103

Describe a time in your relationship where you wished that you had a magical remote control so that you could push the pause button and cause the moment to stretch out longer. Then, share why this time meant so much to you.

Question #104

In the book *Strength Finder 2.0*, Tom Wrath and Donald Clifton describe how experts excel at their craft by building on their strengths. What strengths do you see in your partner? These do not need to be the same strengths described in the book but can be things that he or she excels at in general.

Question #105

In what ways do your strengths and your partner's strengths complement each other?

Question #106

Describe a time that you and your partner utilized your strengths to successfully navigate a dubious situation.

Question #107

What qualities do you admire most in your partner?

Question #108

Tell a story about something you wanted as a teenager, but were not allowed to have. What was it, why were you not allowed to have it, and what did you do?

Question #109

If you were to start an internet blog, what would you write about, and what would you name your site?

Question #110

What questions have you always wanted to ask your parents, but never did? What kept you from asking?

Question #111

Conversations such as "The birds and the bees," can be difficult for both parents and children. What difficult conversation did your parents not have with you, but you wish they did?

Question #112

Describe one of your partner's quirky habits that you find endearing.

Question #113

What is the most exotic food you have ever tasted, and how did you come about trying it?

Question #114

Tell the story about the time you got in the most trouble as a child.

Question #115

It is said that opposites attract. What are some opposites that attract you to your partner?

Question #116

Tell a story about the worst or most embarrassing date you ever went on. When was it, where did you and your date go, and what happened?

Question #117

Tell the story of how you moved out of your parent's house and began living on your own.

Question #118

What is the biggest adventure you and your best friend had together? Describe where you went and what happened.

Question #119

Tell a story about a recent trip or vacation that did not live up to your expectations. What specifically made this experience so disappointing?

Question #120

Imagine that you have the opportunity to eat lunch with anyone currently living, no matter how famous. Who would you eat with, and what would you talk about?

Question #121

What Biblical character is most like you? In what ways are the two of you alike?

Question #122

What is the best April Fool's joke or practical joke that you ever had played on you?

Question #123

Describe the best prank that you ever pulled on someone else.

Question #124

Describe your motivations for going to work. Is it purely financial, or are there other things that attract you to your job?

Question #125

James 1:2 says to count it all joy when you face trials of all kinds. What trials are you currently facing, and how are you finding joy in the midst of them?

Question #126

What was your favorite book during your teenage years, and what did you love about it?

Question #127

Galatians 5:22-23 says, "The fruit of the Spirit is love, joy, peace, patience, kindness, goodness, faithfulness, gentleness, and self-control." Which fruit do you see in your partner's life, and how do you see them manifest?

Question #128

What spiritual fruits are you producing this year? What steps are you taking to nurture these qualities in your life?

Question #129

What were some of your favorite television shows during middle school, and what did you like about them?

Question #130

What is your favorite nickname, and how did you get it?

Question #131

Now that you have reached the end of this book, how will you continue connecting deeply with your partner?

Seasons of Connecting

A friend recently shared how he and his wife spend more time texting than talking. While we both agreed that this is less than ideal, it is also not awful either. This particular friend, like so many people I know, is going through an extraordinarily busy season of life. The bright side is that amidst all of the hustle and bustle, texting keeps him and his wife connected.

I once heard about a Navy Seal, who would write short love notes to his wife, on postcard size paper. He would hide these letters around the house before long deployments, and his wife would discover them over time. This simple idea is creative and ingenious. It is another example of how happy couples connect during busy seasons.

Finally, there is the egg story. Because I heard it many years ago, I only remember a few of the details. The speaker shared how he once wrote short love messages to his wife on every egg in the carton. I don't remember exactly why he did this. There may have been a special occasion involved, or it might have been purely spontaneous. What I do remember is thinking to myself, "One day, after I am married, I am going to try this!" Although I have not done this yet, the idea is in my repertoire of creative connection ideas.

I share these simple stories because they illustrate two important points. First, they show how connecting does not need to be difficult, expensive, or time-consuming. Connecting does not require sending a hundred roses to our loved ones work on Valentine's Day. It can be as simple as giving our partner one rose, on any ordinary day of the week, and doing it simply because connecting for a moment is important.

Second, these stories demonstrate that connecting can be fun. Each story gets progressively more outrageous, and this is how it should be. Connecting is not a task to be completed, nor is it one more item to check off a list. Connecting is more like breathing and blinking, we do it because it is in our genes.

God has hardwired you and me to connect. During some seasons of life, this will be easy. During other seasons, an extra dose of creativity will be required. The important thing is to connect often, connect intimately, and to reconnect quickly every time a disruption occurs.

For you and your partner, accomplishing this might involve diving into another book of conversation starters, sending multiple texts to each other throughout the day, hiding love notes all over your home, or creatively decorating each egg in the carton with loving words of affirmation. The most important thing is to stay connected throughout every season of life.

Wishing you many seasons of creative connecting in the years ahead!

End Notes

1. Genesis 2:18

2. Gottman, John and Silver, Nan. *The Seven Principles for Making Marriage Work: A Practical Guide from the Country's Foremost Relationship Expert*, Harmony Publisher, 2015.

3. Pausch, Randy. *The Last Lecture*, Hyperion Publisher, 2008.

4. Wallace, Kelly. CNN, *Teens spend a 'mind-boggling' 9 hours a day using media, report says. November 3, 2013.* http://www.cnn.com/2015/11/03/health/teens-tweens-media-screen-use-report/

5. A quote from Pam Wright, spoken at a conference on the long-term effects of trauma, recalled from memory.

6. A variation of a quote attributed to Carol Buchner, Maya Angelou, and others.

Thumbs Up
or Thumbs Down

THANK YOU for purchasing this book!

I would love to hear from you! Your feedback not only helps me grow as a writer, but it also helps to get this book into the hands of the readers who need it most. Online reviews are the biggest ways independent authors–like myself–connect with new audiences.

If you loved the book, could you please share your experience? Leaving feedback is as easy as answering any of these questions:

- What did you enjoy about this book?
- What is your most valuable takeaway or insight?
- What have you done differently—or what will you do differently—because of what you read?
- To whom would you recommend this book?

Of course, I am looking for honest reviews. So, if you have a minute to share your experience, good or bad, please consider leaving your review!

I look forward to hearing from you!

Sincerely,

COFFEE SHOP CONVERSATIONS

About The Author

Jed is passionate about helping people live happier, healthier, and more connected lives by having better conversations. He is a husband, father of four girls, a psychology professor, therapist, and a writer.

Jed graduated from Southern California Seminary with a Masters of Divinity and returned to complete a second master's degree in psychology. In his free time, Jed enjoys walking on the beach, reading, and spending time with his incredible family.

Continue the Conversation

    If you enjoyed this book, I would love it if you would <u>leave a review on Amazon</u>. As a new author, your feedback is a huge encouragement and helps books like this one get noticed. It only takes a minute, and every review is greatly appreciated. Oh, and please feel free to stay in touch too!

E-mail: jed@coffeeshopconversations.com

Twitter: <u>@jjurchenko</u>

Facebook: <u>Coffee Shop Conversations</u>

More Creative Conversations

Find this book and others books in the creative conversations series on Amazon.

Deepen your relationship while creating an abundance of happy memories. These creative, insightful, and much-needed conversation starters will help you dive deeper into your relationship and grow in your understanding of each other. This book is for couples who want to defy the odds by building a strong foundation before proclaiming, "I do!"

131 Necessary Conversations before Marriage

More Creative Conversations

Transform your relationship from dull and bland to inspired, passionate, and connected!

This conversation starter's book is for every couple who desires to level-up their relationship. Some questions are purely fun and designed to liven up the mood. Others inspire and encourage you and your partner to dream about the future. Whether you are newly dating or nearing your golden anniversary, these questions are for you!

131 Creative Conversations for Couples

53457044R00037

Made in the USA
Columbia, SC
15 March 2019